The m&m's® BRAND Counting Book

Barbara Barbieri McGrath • Illustrated by Roger Glass

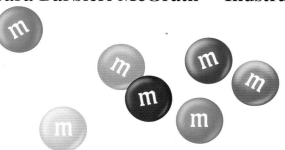

Charlesbridge

The author would like to thank the following people for their assistance and patience: Will M., Roger and Diane G., Albert B. Jr., Joanne B., Jerry P., John B., Mary Ann S., Sue S., Drew Y., M and D, and Karen S.

Published by Charlesbridge Publishing
85 Main Street
Watertown, MA 02472
(617) 926-0329
www.charlesbridge.com

Printed in South Korea
(sc) 15 14 13 12 11 10 9 8 7 6 5 4 3 2 1
(hc) 10 9 8 7 6 5 4 3 2 1

Library of Congress Cataloging-in-Publication Data

McGrath, Barbara Barbieri, 1954-
    The "M&M'S"® brand counting book / Barbara Barbieri McGrath ; illustrated by Roger Glass.
    p. cm.
    Summary: Uses "M&M'S"® Chocolate Candies to introduce counting, addition, subtraction, sets, colors, and shapes.
    ISBN 1-57091-367-6 (reinforced library use)—ISBN 1-57091-368-4 (softcover)
    1. Counting—Juvenile literature. 2. Colors—Juvenile literature.
[1. Counting. 2. Mathematics. 3. Color.] I. Title: "M&M'S"® brand counting book. II. Title: "M&M'S"® brand counting book. III. Glass, Roger, ill. IV. Title.
    QA113 .M3937 2002
    513.2'11—dc21
    [E]   2001006628

This book is dedicated with love to Will, Emily, and W. Louis—B. B. M.

With love to Di—R. G.

Pour out your candies.
Get ready, get set.
This counting book
is the tastiest yet!

Read all the color words
from left to right,
Blue, green, orange,
yellow, red, brown. . .
a pretty sight.

Blue! Green! Orange! Yellow! Red! Brown

This certainly is a colorful mix!
Now sort them as I do, and count up to six.

One blue

1
One

Two green

Two

Three orange

Let's go!

Three

Four yellow

4

Four

Five red

5

Five

Six brown

Good show!

Six

Let's count to twelve now.
That's a dozen, you know.

Keep the six brown.
Push the others aside.

Please use these pictures
and words as your guide.

Now add a blue to make seven. . .
that's great!

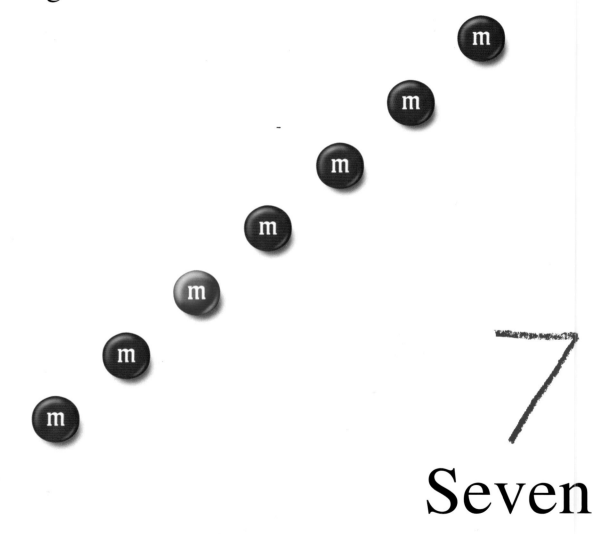

7
Seven

Put a green near the middle.
Now you have eight!

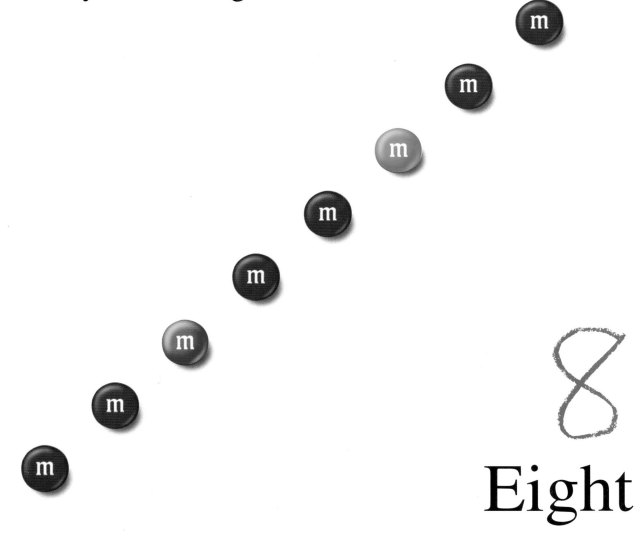

8

Eight

Add a red to your group to make nine,
and then. . .

9
Nine

Add the orange and
now we've already reached ten!

10
Ten

To get eleven, add a yellow one now.

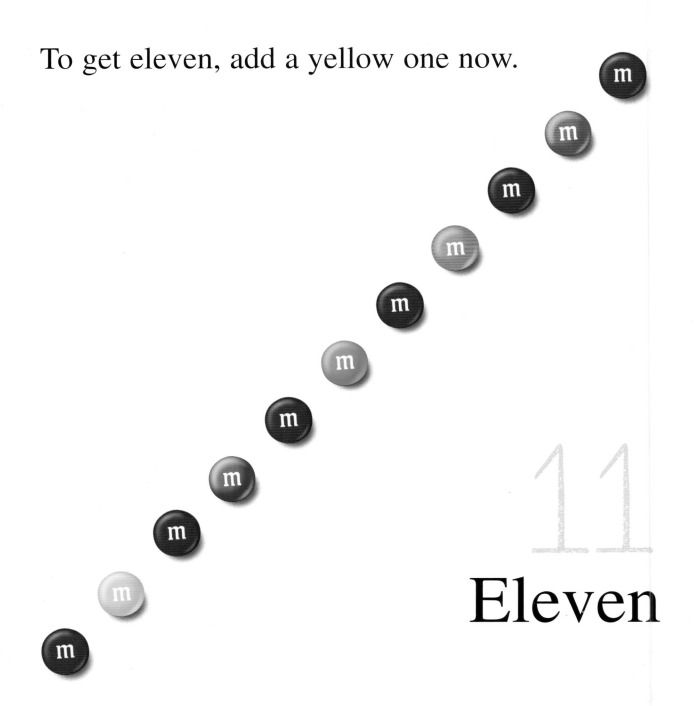

11

Eleven

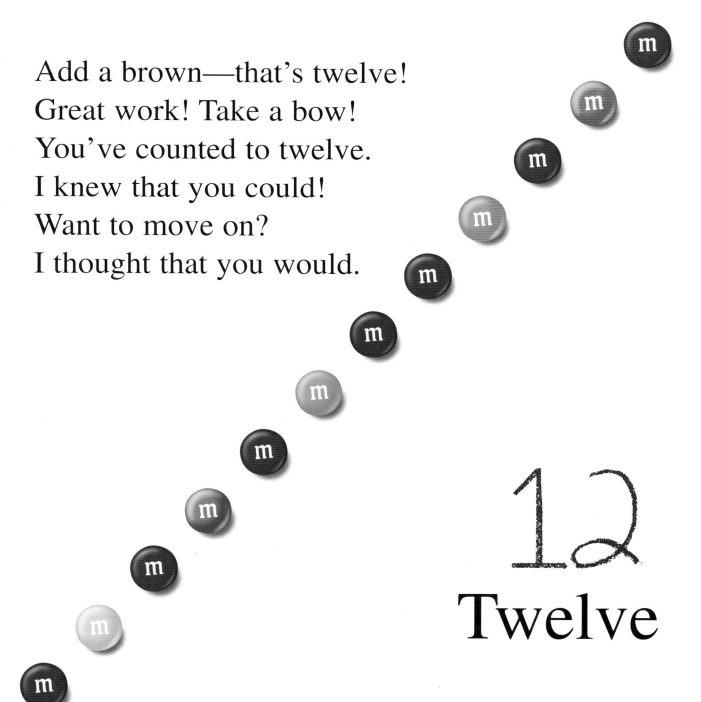

Add a brown—that's twelve!
Great work! Take a bow!
You've counted to twelve.
I knew that you could!
Want to move on?
I thought that you would.

12
Twelve

Now put the twelve candies
in a long line.
We call this a set.
You're doing just fine!

1 set
One set

Make six groups of two.
That's easy for you.
What does this make?
Six sets of two!

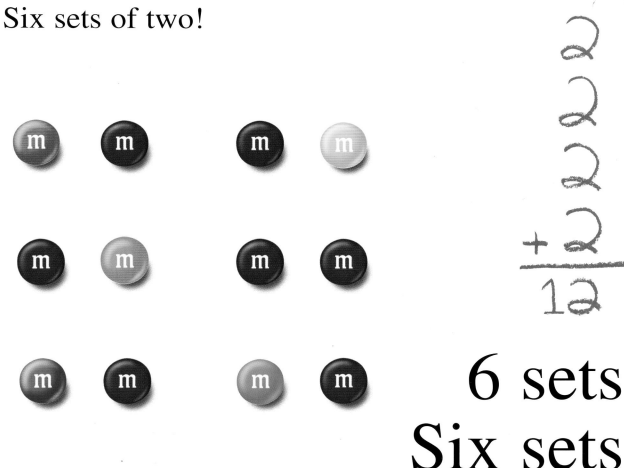

$$
\begin{array}{r}
2 \\
2 \\
2 \\
2 \\
2 \\
+\ 2 \\
\hline
12
\end{array}
$$

6 sets
Six sets

Change them around to make three sets of four. Count them. How many? Still twelve and no more!

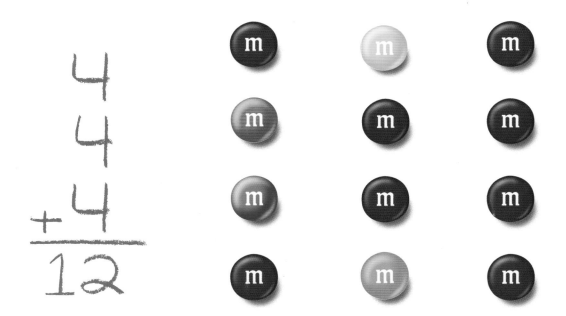

$$\begin{array}{r} 4 \\ 4 \\ + 4 \\ \hline 12 \end{array}$$

3 sets

Three sets

Now it is time to make four sets of three.
There are still only twelve, as you can see.

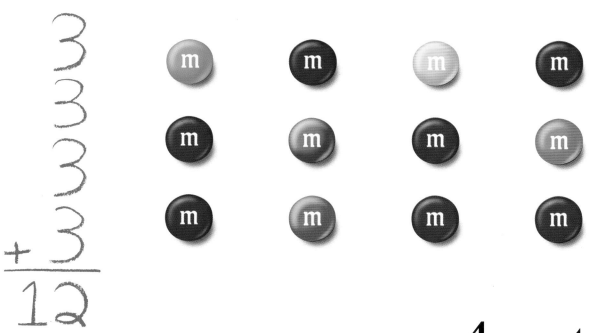

3
3
3
+3
12

4 sets
Four sets

Make two sets of six now.
How did you do?
You did that so well—
let's start something new.

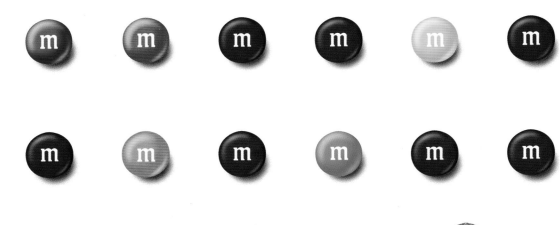

2 sets
Two sets

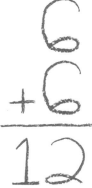

Shape the twelve candies, please, into a square.
A square has four sides.
Please count them with care.

Square

Change the square to a circle, the big round kind.
A circle's beginning is so hard to find.

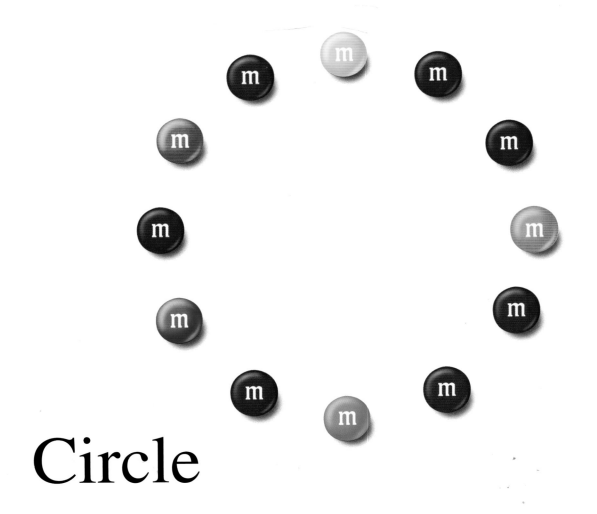

Circle

Let's make a triangle before we stop.
Give it three sides and a point on the top.

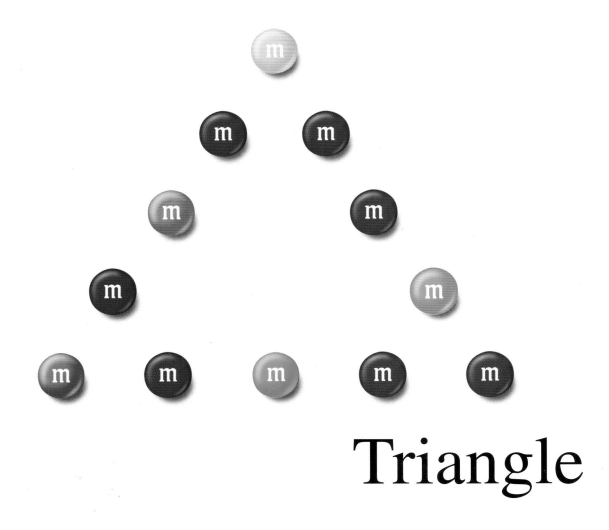

Triangle

Now comes the part that
will be the most fun.
We'll start to subtract—
so eat the blue one.

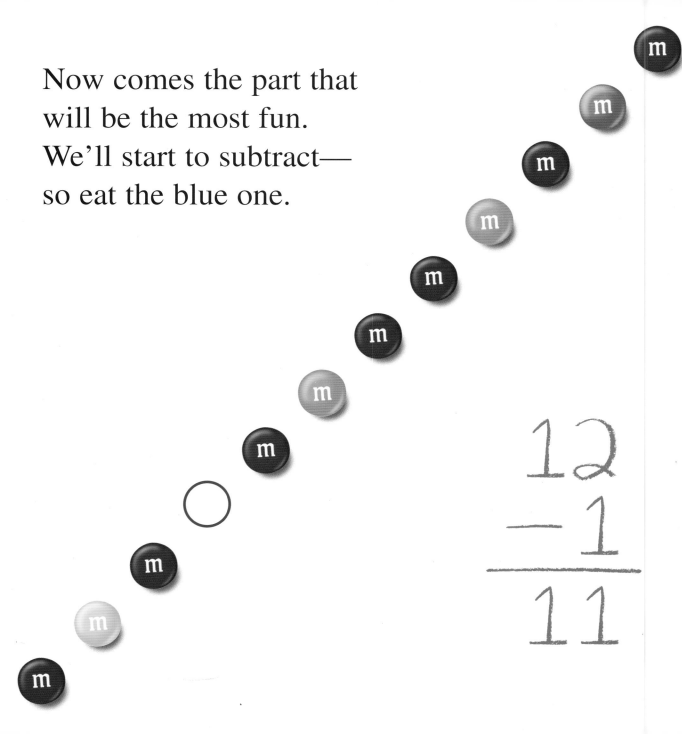

12
−1
———
11

Count and you'll find
you now have eleven.
Next eat the brown.
Go on, eat all seven!

$$\begin{array}{r} 11 \\ -7 \\ \hline 4 \end{array}$$

Now you have four left.
So please eat the green.
The orange, red, and yellow
still can be seen.

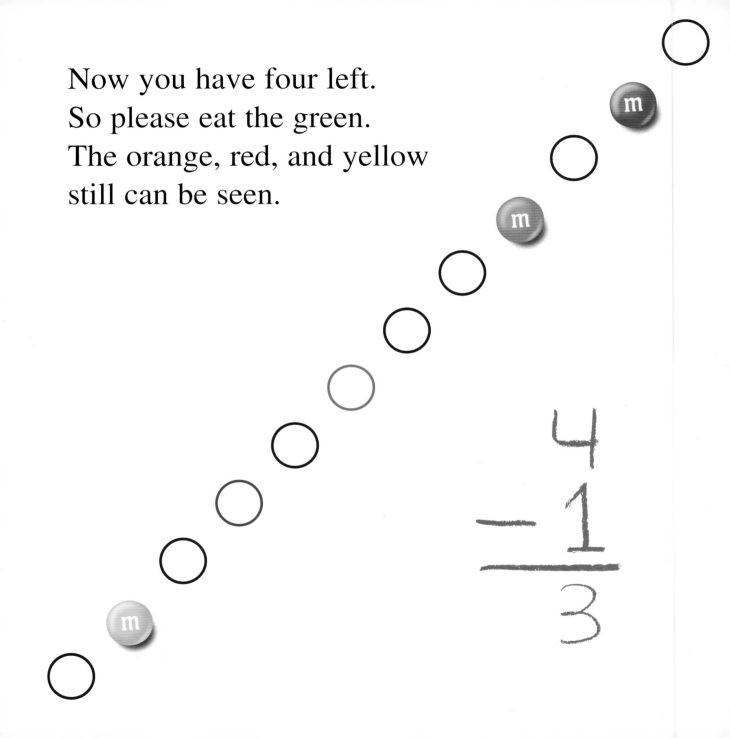

$$\frac{4}{-1}{3}$$

Next eat the orange one,
and after you do. . .
How many are left?
Oh dear, only two!

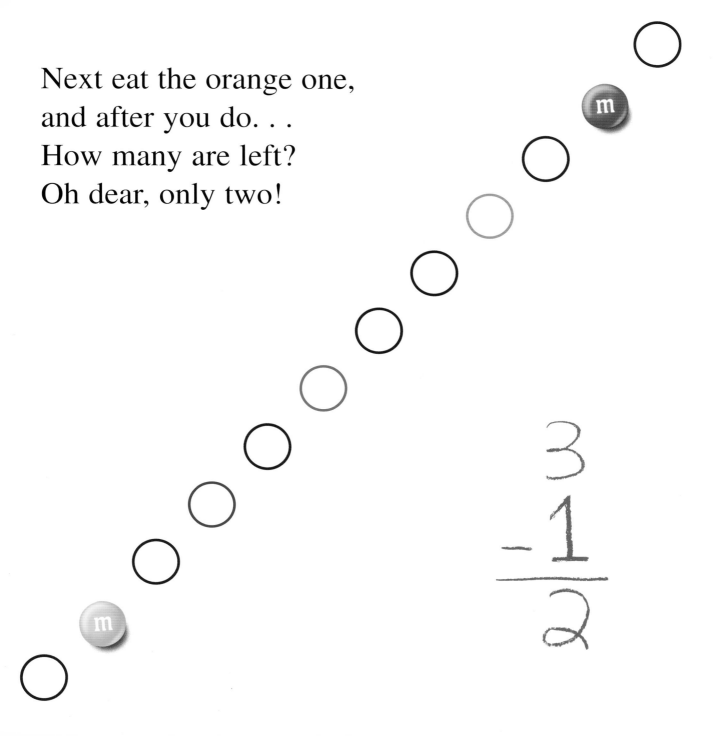

$$\begin{array}{r} 3 \\ -1 \\ \hline 2 \end{array}$$

Now eat the yellow—
it's second to last.
Counting like this
makes the time fly by fast.

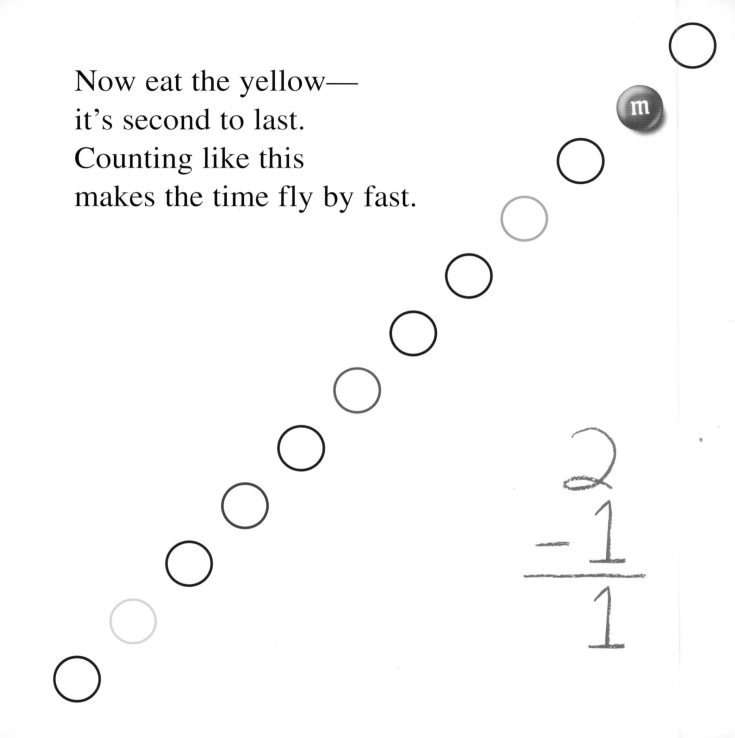

How many are left?
You're right, only one.
Eat the red that is last.
Now you are done!

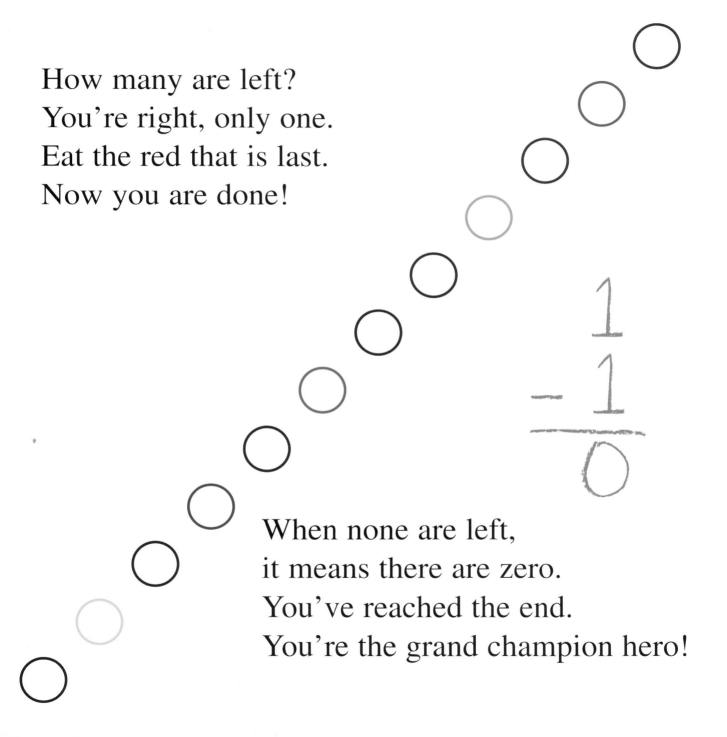

$$\begin{array}{r} 1 \\ -\ 1 \\ \hline 0 \end{array}$$

When none are left,
it means there are zero.
You've reached the end.
You're the grand champion hero!

You've done a great job,
and we're so proud of you.
To help you remember,
here's your review!

Colors:

 Blue   Green   Brown

 Orange   Yellow   Red

Shapes:

Square   Triangle   Circle

Numbers:

1	**2**	**3**
One	Two	Three
4	**5**	**6**
Four	Five	Six
7	**8**	**9**
Seven	Eight	Nine
10	**11**	**12**
Ten	Eleven	Twelve

The sets of 12:

1 set   • • • • • • • • • • • •

2 sets   • • • • • •   • • • • • •

3 sets   • • • •   • • • •   • • • •

4 sets   • • •   • • •   • • •   • • •

6 sets   • •   • •   • •   • •   • •   • •